Jake's Dinner

Contents

Shops	page 5
Transport	page 6
Milk	page 7
Carrots	page 8
Fish fingers	page 12
Cake	page 14

Written by Fiona Undrill
Illustrated by Sarah Hoyle

T0351218

On his plate, Jake has three fish fingers, and eight bits of carrot.

He has a cup of milk too.

I need to explain to Jake how food gets to us.

Jake says food comes from shops.

Big trucks take food to the shops.
Lots of food comes from farms.

Milk

Thank you, Mrs Cow!

Some farms have cows.
Cows make milk.

What little seeds!

Carrots come from farms too.
The seeds go in the soil.

They get lots of sun and rain.
They get bigger and bigger ...

9

The carrots come out of the soil.

We made today's carrots with Dad.

Fish have fins and tails but no fingers!

Boats bring the fish to land.
The fish is cut up, and made into finger shapes.

Jake makes a cake.

Jake says he did all the weighing, mixing, cooking and finishing.

Think! How did we get all this?